Beautiful Life

Zara Ali

Presentation by *BookLeaf Publishing*

Web: www.bookleafpub.com

E-mail: info@bookleafpub.com

ISBN: 9789395755085

First edition 2022

DEDICATION

I would like to dedicate this book to everyone who has a dream or goal they wish to pursue further. This is to motivate and encourage them that they can also go very far in life.

Lastly that no matter how many setbacks or problems they face on the path of their goals- if they never give up, they will eventually get there and be successful one day.

ACKNOWLEDGEMENT

The completion of this book could not have been
possible without the encouragement and help
from my parents Munir Ali and Farhat Ali.
They have always motivated me and supported
me to follow my dreams and meet my goals.
Everything I am today is because of God and
then my parents.

I would also like to thank my husband Haseeb
Ahmad who has always praised my writing and
encouraged me to take this dream forward in my
life. He has read many of my poems and
provided feedback.

PREFACE

In this book of poems, I intend for the reader to take a journey through the various experiences of human life. The topics of these poems are quite expansive, so there is a poem which everyone can relate to. And if not a specific poem, there will be certain parts which people can relate to.

This book will open some hearts and minds and allow the reader to dive in deeper to themselves and others. Please note the topics included in these poems are all my personal views and opinions gained through various books, people, experiences, my travels and overall life.

The Lessons in Nature

Nature communicates many languages
Everyone can listen but only a few can
understand
The way the sea revisits the shore repeatedly
Which makes arrival and departure take place so
smoothly
The tree branches which sway with the tune of
the wind
Doing a dance with each stroke
The leaves landing on the ground
Ever so gracefully and selflessly
Creating space for the new arrivals
The blue sky accompanied by the white, gentle,
soft and loving clouds
The sunrise introducing us to a new beginning
The sunset showing us that endings are not
always painful and tragic
There is something beautiful about the fresh
smell of the rain
The sweet soil having a bath each time the rain
brings its presence
The sound of rain is therapy for the ears
Nature teaches us that we can all be very
different
Yet belong to the same garden

The roses, the tulips, the daises, the green grass,
and the unique plants
They never fight over who is more beautiful and
who is better
They simply exist with their confidence and
uniqueness intact, leaving an impact on those
around them
There is a life story from the planting of the
seed, the growth, the struggles and challenges
and then the final result
In order to see these things, we need to just sit,
observe and stop for a moment to absorb the
natural world around us
There is a peace, a hope, a dream lingering in
these places telling us to continue
Telling us that our purpose is not to get lost in
this superficial life
Just eat, sleep, work and die in the end
Surely, we must have another purpose
Nature teaches us beauty, joy, sadness, loss,
love, faith, purpose, a process and a way of
living, all in very simple ways
If you use your five senses in nature closely
You will find many answers to questions you
were and were not aware of

Old Souls

Some of us stand out from the very beginning
It may be the way we become emotional at a
very young age
Often as a result of things which others feel we
could never understand due to our age
But what if some of us do understand?
What if we understand even deeper than those
older than us?
Even a baby can get emotional when it sees a
baby kitten
Age is just a number
The soul goes way beyond our age
Old souls are deep and mysterious like the ocean
They value truth, kindness, honesty, compassion,
and respect
Old souls love the simple things in life
Nature, family, a small home full of peace and
love
Old souls are emotional, sentimental and oh so
nostalgic!
The wisdom of old souls cannot be replaced
As they hold onto their values and morals tightly

Eyes

I have seen all kinds of eyes
Some of them shine bright like the moon on a
dark night
I often wonder to myself if their eyes shine so
brightly
How much light must their soul carry?
Other eyes shine like there is an ocean inside
waiting to be discovered
The rest of them often carry a deep pain, a
brokenness, a yearning for love
All eyes regardless of their traits tell a story
And some carry their story
Their whole life without ever being asked
Tell me your story?
Share with me the emotions you hide so deeply
in that heart of yours
I want to hear the good, the bad and the ugly
I want to know how your eyes can be so full of
love and mercy
When life has been anything but kind to you
What kind of heart did God bless you with?
That even in your own wrenching pain you want
to make sure
Everyone else is doing, okay?

My Everything

All this life is a story between You and I
Every person, every experience, every test,
every emotion
Takes me back to you
Your pure and unconditional love
I mean just look at how You created me
And every human being
With such detail, perfection and magnificence
You are the best Artist and Creator of absolute
beauty
All the artists in the world are put to shame in
front of Your Creations
Look at how You created the flower
It starts from the small seed in the earth
With rain, sun and wind
It transforms into a work of art
Not only pleasing to the eyes
Pleasing to all of our senses
They say we have five senses but really You
created us with many more
All my senses recognise and take me back
To my only Reality and my only Home
You

Love

If I were to share the most significant aspect of
life
Without a doubt it would be Love
Everything has a need
The body needs food
The soul needs peace and prayer
The mind needs to keep busy
The heart needs love
Love is where the story all began
First God made a plan to create us with Love
Out of His Love He created for us this beautiful
World
We were then created from nothing, and blessed
with caregivers to meet our need for love
Then we continue to search our whole lives to be
seen and to feel love from others
All to feel some kind of attachment, a bond, a
feeling of love
Love is often found in the small gestures,
communications, and acts of kindness
We are all just simple beings at heart
Truly we do not care for worldly aspects
But in our search for love

We give love to materialistic things which were
only meant to be used, not depended on
We use people who were only meant to be loved
and depended on to a certain extent

Inner Child

We all have a child within us
This child is a very simple part of us
It loves to play and have fun
It only asks for pure love and time
It forms a large part of our personality traits
Some of these traits are kindness, honesty and
curiosity
Notice how as adults we often enjoy what we
loved as children
As they bring us back to some of our happy
memories
Eating ice cream
Playing at the beach in the water and sand
Watching movies and cartoons
Swimming, Playing and being outdoors
In fact, you would be surprised to know
How much our inner child actually affects us in
our daily lives
Maybe that's why we feel so deeply about
certain situations
Or we get emotional when we see an injustice
taking place
This is also why we love children and babies so
much

They have a gentleness, an innocence, a love
and an awe for life
Our inner child recognises itself in others
It is constantly thinking and feeling
What if that was me?
And often it feels that is me
When we live a life from the soul
We give that child freedom to be who they are

Mother

I have often heard people say
You cannot judge some experiences until you
have experienced them
Motherhood is one of those experiences in my
life
I knew that I was given a precious gift, a miracle
A responsibility, for a new life which would be
dependent on God then on me
I never knew that through this child I would also
be reborn
The day I gave birth to my little miracle
I felt my heart would burst with love
My mind, just could not believe that I was
blessed with such a gift
This poem is not just about me
It is about all the mothers out there
Whether they gave birth, adopted, fostered or
have maternal instincts
The mother is a home within a home
They say a mother works without any pay
I disagree
To see your child smile at you with pure love in
their eyes
When they search for you in their sleep and their
breathing gets relaxed as soon as they find you

The entertainment they provide free of charge
Even if that means the whole tub of Vaseline is
on their hands and face
These aspects are some of the greatest rewards
for a mother
Being a mother is a great blessing which comes
with a lot of hard work
God compared His love to a mother's love
By saying that His love is greater than a mother's
love for her child
I often reflect on how deep a mother's love is
My mind cannot comprehend how deep and
beautiful Gods love must be
For He created such a beautiful creation the
Mother

Father

Although a father often spends most of his time
outside the home
Working hard to earn for his family
His love is no less than a mothers
He shows his love through many different ways
He brings home his child's favourite chocolate or
a new toy
Just to see his child smile
He saves up every penny to build a home for his
family
Often working 2 jobs to cover his bills and
expenses
A father makes great sacrifices for his children
However, you will never hear him saying a word
about this sacrifice
It is because his love is so strong for his children
He may not verbally express his love often
But his smile for his child tells the whole story
The best kind of fathers are those who you can
chat to like a friend
The ones who always have a joke and laugh up
their sleeve
They have a story to tell, and honestly if
someone else were to tell the same story

It would bore us to death
Some fathers have a light in their heart and a
presence which fills up a room
When they are not there everything feels empty
and lifeless
A father holds a child's hand temporally
but his/her heart forever

Rain

It seems after the rain there is always
This calmness, this serenity, this peace
It's like during that storm
During that rain
It poured down so heavily
It destroyed many things
But it also cleared the way for a lot of things
It cleared the pathway of leaves, twigs
The wind moved these items
The rainfall cleansed many things
Like the oceans, rivers
Just like tears cleanse our hearts
Just like the rain comes
There is a peace, a serenity
If you're going through a difficult situation in
your life
There will come a calmness, a peace
After the difficulty
But also, with the difficulty
You just need to wait a bit longer
Patience does not come without hardship
Your days will end
Your hardships will end
Your circumstances will change just like the rain

When you are in the rain, you feel like nothing is
going to ever change
The downpour will never stop
And you will continue to get soaked in the rain,
in your pain
But there is a period where it becomes lighter
Or it just stops altogether
Just like your difficulties
So do not ever lose hope
Hope is what keeps us going
One day the rain will dry, and you will be sitting
in the beautiful sunshine
The darkness will leave, and the light will come
to be

A bird

If I could be any animal
I would choose to be a bird
Resilient yet soft hearted
Beautiful yet so very humble
Different yet unique
Free in the sky, enjoying the scenery and
weather
Living freely in nature, with a different home
each time
My heart and soul rising towards the sky with
my body towards my Creator
Not confined to four walls in a busy, polluted
city
I would love to enjoy nature up close
Breathing in the fresh air whilst absorbing the
stunning views around me
I could fly for miles and miles
Travelling to some of the most beautiful
destinations of the world
I would try to communicate with the birds in
other countries learning their culture and their
language
I would build a nest for me and my family
From the twigs I find on my flying trips
I would fly out to find food for my family

And feed my children so lovingly with my
mouth
When they would be ready, I would teach them
how to fly
On a warm day I would bathe in the ocean and
nearby lakes
And enjoy the shade under the wide and
beautiful trees
I would look out for and be compassionate to all
the other creatures above and below me
There would be struggles and hardships
But my freedom to fly wherever I wanted
Would surpass every hardship I would
experience

The journey of life

We are all on a journey
I call it the journey of life
We learn knowledge through reading
We learn how to live through our experiences
But reading can never teach us what we learn
through our life experiences
The good and the bad we always learn
In this journey we will be faced with a lot of
different experiences
Meet people who will love us, hurt us, be jealous
People who come into our lives and stay
Others who play their part in our story then
leave
They all serve a specific purpose
Some change us for the better and some for the
worse
But in the process, they are all a part of making
us into who we are
Who we were always meant to be
This journey of life
Will make us smile, laugh and sometimes even
cry
But we need all these emotions to truly feel this
life in full
Imagine if our life was easy all the time

We would never appreciate our blessings
The strange thing is we only value something
before we gain it and after we lose it

Change

Change is a part of everyday life
How the day transforms into night
The sun departs to welcome the rain
The way the seasons change so effortlessly
We humans are creatures of change
We were made to change and adapt to change
Although that doesn't always make it easy
We are nostalgic, sentimental, emotional and
become attached too easily
We hang onto anyone or any experience which
brought us joy
This often explains why we visit the same places
Over and over again
We may not even like some of those places
But in those places, we have beautiful memories
with some special people
We know we need to make changes in certain
areas of our life
Yet we still continue to hold onto the old
because it is familiar
It is comfortable and feels safe for us
We fear going into the unknown because it will
be different
But we fail to realise it may be much brighter,
much better for us

The comfort zone is where many dreams come
to die
We should always try new foods, new places,
new groups
And much more new bigger experiences if we
have such opportunities
And hey if we do not like the new, we can
always go back to the old
It will be right there on the sofa waiting for us to
come back
But would you rather be lying on the sofa or be
out there chasing your dreams?

Simplicity

A simple life is a blessed life
Have you ever visited a very poor country or
someone who owns very little wealth
You will often notice even though they have
very little in terms of materialism and wealth
Their hearts are full of peace
They thank God for everything they have been
blessed with
Despite having one bedroom in which five
children sleep
A bathroom miles away
Water access is limited, and they must walk
miles to get this water
But they have one very important quality that
people in the developed world often lack
They live a very simple and humble life
Okay so you may argue circumstances force
them to live such a life
Thats true in many cases
But nothing forces them to have such a positive
attitude
To be compassionate, kind and loving despite
their experiences
To be so grateful and patient with the life they
live

Maybe when you have little it allows you to
appreciate each blessing in full
And when you have more, you just forget to be
grateful for your blessings
Until you are just trying to satisfy the ego and
the soul becomes buried among all these items
Aha!
Maybe that's the secret
The people who are simple and lead a simple life
Live from the soul rather than the ego
In other words, the soul thrives on pure love, so
it only needs love, compassion, respect, trust and
all the similar qualities
The ego is just so desperate to feel love that it
searches for it in all the wrong places;
addictions, wealth, materialistic items, showing
off and so on and so forth

Kindness

Some of the best things about kindness are
It is free yet both the giver and the taker receive
something beautiful in return
It is done with this thought in mind
That in this situation, it could be me and often
that it is me
To the woman who seems troubled at heart a
smile could have saved her life that day
To the elderly man who was struggling to cross
the road with his frail legs but the young person
who stopped to help him could have restored his
faith in humanity
To the friend who needed a warm hug that day
because of their pet cat dying
To the rubbish sweeper who most people just
ignore needed those words of "Thank you, what
you do really means a lot to me and this world"
To the child who started their first day of
nursery, who was given a little flower from the
street to say "have a good first day"
A heart full of kindness is a beautiful heart full
of love, a soul full of light and eyes full of
passion
For this world and its people and all living
things

If I had to choose between being intelligent and
being kind, I would choose being kind
Our intelligence which is a gift can help us to
reach our dreams and ambitions
But our kindness can help others reach their
dreams and ambitions
With our kindness we can change the world one
step at a time
I will be proud of my children's achievements
However, I will be prouder of their ability to
share a smile, say a kind word, stand up to a
bully for the new child
To sit and befriend the lonely child and to share
love with every human and living thing in this
world
Kindness does not cost anything but to be kind is
a gift

The Ego and the Soul

The ego and the soul
are polar opposites in every way
Except one
They both seek love
The ego seeks love in the external world
Whereas the soul seeks love in the internal
world
The differences between them both are
extremely vast
The ego operates on fear
Whereas the soul thrives on the unknown
The ego seeks instant temporary pleasure,
thinking it is forever
The soul seems permanent peace, knowing it
will be forever
The ego is easily impressed with the fake
aspects of life- wealth, materialistic items,
brands, names, celebrities
The soul is harder to impress it only becomes
impressed with the real- Love, compassion,
honesty, truth
The ego is all about me
The soul wants to think of others as well
The ego only sees what it can gain
The soul never gets tired of giving

I know it seems as if I have painted the ego as
being the problem
But the truth is that the ego is the part of us
which connects to our inner child
However, when it is wounded it seeks love in the
wrong places
The wounded ego will do everything and
anything to have its needs met
But if the ego is taken care of through providing
safety, security, consistency and love
It can also heal to become much healthier
And then instead of the ego running the show of
our life
The ego can take a back seat and let the soul
lead it where it needs to go
Both the soul and the ego are important, but they
have to be managed correctly

Open minded

Being open minded means understanding that
We are all different in many ways
It means to respect people's differences without
rejecting our own
It requires us to have a respect and love for
others
It means to keep an open mind about the things
we know and see about others
But also, to read and educate ourselves about the
aspects of ourselves and others,
We do not understand easily or understand at all
It means that instead of believing the stereotypes
We go directly to the source; we meet the group
who have been stereotyped
We spend a day with them in their life or we ask
them questions until we understand
We become brave, we question, we speak up, we
stand up, we go against the majority, if we need
to
Being open minded does not mean we agree
with everything and anything we are told
It means that our respect and love for that
person/group is not affected by our emotions

We do not always require to speak up about
everything and anything which bothers us
Some things require a deep observation and
silence
Others require words and actions
I guess it's impossible to always be open minded
But we can always try to be as much as is
possible
Maybe the quiet and shy person you see has
been betrayed in the past
The person you see living such a peaceful and
happy life went through a lot to get where they
are today
Maybe the student is late because they are
helping a younger special needs sibling to their
class
And maybe just maybe we are more in need of
opening our minds, than judging straight away
what we see on the surface
The surface is sometimes nothing compared to
what goes on within

Peace

Whether we like to admit it or not
We are all searching for peace
This is a lifelong search, which involves
Many healthy and unhealthy ways of dealing
with our pain and searching for peace
Some take drugs and drink alcohol
Others begin to search for peace in another
human being
And some turn towards faith and religion
But inside us all exists a deep pain, an inner
turmoil, a void
That void can only be filled with Gods Eternal
Love
Any other peace we seek is temporary, in fact
this whole world is temporary
And many of Gods Signs and Creations in this
world show us this time and time again
Even the beautiful flower eventually dries up
and dies
How can we seek peace in things which do not
last?
Or which cause us some level of harm?
Your question is what about Yoga or meditation
or similar aspects?

These can be a means to gain peace, but the truth
is that then we begin to think peace can come
from us
When really, we do not hold such a capacity or
position that we can bring ourselves peace
Infact we cannot even self soothe as babies we
need a caregiver to teach us how to self soothe
So, the human is always dependent on God
whether they like to admit this or not
And peace only comes from knowing, loving
and remembering God in all forms
As God is the Creator, He holds the secret for
peace

The ocean

If you go to the beach one day
Just
Sit
In
Complete
Silence
Listen
To
The
Ocean
It has a language and tune of its own
Stillness of the sand beside the constant
movement of the waves
The way the waves come out and back in again
sometimes gently other times with more force
The way our feet melt into the soft sand and then
the ocean flows onto our feet
Making us feel like we are Home
The sound of the waves reminding me of the
sound inside a mothers womb
Peaceful, safe, protected, warm and loved
God has a way of showing us His love through
nature

He is the best teacher because He has placed so
many experiences, examples, lessons, learning
points in the natural world around us
Sometimes we just need to step away from our
busy and packed lives
Turn off the phones and just visit the ocean
You may have come troubled, not knowing what
to feel or what to say
But as soon as the ocean says hello in fact even
goodbye
Its like those worries vanish as the tide goes
back in
I have never heard the ocean speak yet it says so
much to me in its silence, its waves, its presence,
its peace
Lastly different parts of the ocean can represent
the human life experience
The flowing of the waves like our tears
sometimes gentle and other times with more
pressure
The way the waves go in and back out again,
representing our emotional state
Sometimes our emotions overspill covering the
whole sand, just like the sea
Whilst at other times our emotions are constant
and go in and out ever so slightly just like the
sea

Lastly the depth of the ocean can represent our
deepest thoughts, words, and feelings often
buried under the ocean waiting to be discovered
There are other aspects of us that are so deep, so
intense; others must dive in deeper to really
understand and get to know us

Education

Education can mean a lot of things
But for me education is not limited to having
gone to school or university
Having good grades or a degree does not make a
person more educated or intelligent
Sure, it is always positive to work hard and
strive in anything we take on
But the education system is often not catered for
the analytical/critical thinkers
Much of it places students into a box
But what if a student wants to be inside a maze
But really some people have other skills and
knowledge, if they were to be confined to good
grades or a degree their confidence could be lost
forever
If your education makes you a better person
overall, then your education has been successful
But if you still throw rubbish on the ground,
Disrespect or look down to those on a lower
income or struggling in some way and are
dishonest with others
What have you really gained from such an
education?

I think some of the poorest people have a better
education and some of them have never even
had an opportunity to go to school
Education is seen in your actions, words,
behaviour and self-discipline
It shows in the way you respect yourself and
others
We can educate ourselves daily through faith,
observation, deep reflection, reading and
understanding even one sentence a day
Growing and developing ourselves by working
on our weaknesses and feeling grateful for
strengths, travelling and meeting up with all
kinds of people in all walks of life

Truth

Always tell the truth
One of those things which we are taught at a
young age
Yet as life goes on, we actually realise
This life is nothing but a beautiful lie
The celebrities who are airbrushed to
"perfection"
I say perfection but how long will this fake
beauty last?
Then we lie to ourselves that we are not getting
older, or I don't have any grey hairs yet
What if we just embraced our grey hairs?
Our wrinkles, our leaving eyesight, our sore
legs, our disappearing hearing
And just admitted to ourselves that we are
getting old
But why is that something so shameful?
Every age and every stage carries its own
beauty, grace and speciality
Be brave, be grateful, be comfortable in your
own skin
There is truly no one like you in this beautiful
world

Sensitive

Society always says sensitivity is a weakness
When actually it is one of the biggest strengths
out there
A person has to be really brave to be sensitive in
a world which can often be very unkind
Sensitive people actually carry a lot of gifts
They are often very creative, passionate, witty
and knowledgeable
Sensitive people make the best leaders, social
workers, teachers and parents
They are often loved by children, animals, the
elderly and anyone who they cross their paths
with
It's because they always try to speak to people at
their level
Their love and care can be seen in the bright
shining light in their eyes
They have a soul full of fire, a heart full of
compassion and love and a deep and beautiful
embrace
They are emotional, sentimental and get attached
easily
They enjoy the simple small blessings and
experiences in life

Like picking up some small seashells to bring
back from the beach
Or their daily hot chocolate they have from their
favourite cafe or even better homemade
They truly live from the soul so effortlessly and
confidently
They truly love for others what they would for
themselves
They would give away what they have in a
heartbeat
Even if that means they will have to do without
Sensitive people bring a special kind of beauty
and vibe which can be felt by everyone around
them including those who cannot see or hear
them